Echoes Of War

Donald Dunn

Published by Donald Dunn, 2024.

While every precaution has been taken in the preparation of this book, the publisher assumes no responsibility for errors or omissions, or for damages resulting from the use of the information contained herein.

ECHOES OF WAR

First edition. March 12, 2024.

ISBN: 979-8224353552

Written by Donald Dunn.

Table of Contents

Dedication

Dedication

Dedication of this book goes to my family. They have sacrificed so much throughout my career. They have stood by my side through all the hard times. I genuinely want to thank my wife. She is a powerful woman, a fantastic mother, and my best friend. I want to thank my children as well. I know you did not know me prior to the military; however, you have seen the changes in me from the military. I hope this book can answer some questions and remind you how much I love each of you.

To my son, Johnathan, I am sorry for the years we lost together. Failing to grasp that genuine happiness does not come from material possessions, I tirelessly strived for our betterment while being away from the military. Last, I apologize for projecting my own issues onto you. I can't bring back that time, but I truly hope that this book will give you answers. Mostly, I wanted to tell you, as I have watched you grow up, that you are the father I wish I was. I am very proud of you and will always love you.

To my daughter, who always wanted me there on July 22, between the Army constantly having me gone, I missed the one day a year that you loved more than anything. Regardless of saying I am sorry for that and wishing I could have changed that, it will remain unchanged. I apologize for not being present to you. I am very proud of you and everything that you have accomplished. You're the first to get a college degree among us. You are raising four children and supporting your husband with all the things he is trying to accomplish, not to mention also working a full-time job. Proud of you does not describe how I feel. I wish I could have taken some credit for your success, but the truth goes to your mom.

To my wife, I wanted to improve your life because you had a tough childhood. I feel I started on that path, and I was trying my best to give you a nice safe home to raise our children. As my best friend and soul mate, you are everything to me. I understand how I lost track. The separation between us, as the years passed, was my fault. My perception became distorted, and I started sensing hostility from the world. I juggled two lives, failing in both. To keep up appearances, I acted like everything was fine at work and at home. I apologize, but you were the reason our kids turned out great. Your dedication to making sure they had clothes and healthy meals and helping them with their homework. You knew everything about our kids and always saw their full potential. You are incredible, and I thank you every day.

I dedicate this to all my military comrades, my brothers, and sisters. Their memories are my strength. Unforgettable are the bonds of brotherhood and sisterhood we shared. The sacrifices their families made to allow us to do our jobs are truly amazing.

Introduction: Who I Was Before Joining the Military

Amid extraordinary circumstances, this story focuses on an ordinary man and not a superhero. It begins much like anyone's life, not marked by a tragic childhood but a relatively happy one. Although my mother abandoned me at two and my father handed me over to my grandparents, their love surrounded me and care. We were not affluent, yet we never lacked essentials: food, clothing, and a sheltering roof. This narrative unfolds the life I have lived, a journey of transformation and resilience.

In order for my children to understand my evolution, I am driven to write this book. It aims to illuminate the factors shaping the person I am today. My wife, bearing more than her share, has been a pillar. This endeavor also stems from a growing fear of memory loss. The fading recollections of my children's favorite toys, the shows they watched, and their infant faces spurred me to document my experiences. I hope this book offers solace and guidance to others grappling with PTSD and TBI, perhaps aiding families in recognizing and addressing these conditions early. I know most veterans don't share the tragedies that happen while being deployed. The change in behavior and personality confuses families, hindering their understanding.

Illustrating the profound impact of my illness, the essence of this book starts from my early years. I intend to reveal the person I was and the changes that ensued. While many books discuss PTSD, few capture the gradual onset and progression of its symptoms. PTSD manifests diversely, with each person experiencing unique triggers and signs. Contrary to dramatic portrayals on TV, it involves subtle changes like self-isolation, mood swings, and impulsive decisions. These less conspicuous symptoms can be just as significant to be noticed.

Chapter 1: Shaped by Challenges: The Path to Finding My Strength

Learning lessons as young adults shapes us into the adults we become. My life has clarified that this truth is true. Before delving deeper, I want to clarify something: the individuals I refer to as Mom and Dad are, in fact, my grandparents. My biological mother left when I was two, turning to prostitution in Colorado. My father, too young to raise a child, joined the Navy and relinquished his parental rights to my grandparents. I maintained contact with my biological father until his passing. However, my relationship with my biological mother was distant. I last sought her out at 18, only to realize that giving birth doesn't inherently make one a mother. My children later met her but never knew her as their grandmother. I chose not to introduce her as such, believing in earning the title of a mother. Despite these circumstances, my story isn't one of sorrow but of a blessed childhood, vastly preferable to what might have been with my biological parents.

The narrative begins in 1987, being the earliest of my detailed memories. My best friend, Randy, and I were living our best lives in Valley Springs, a small town in Northern California. I filled my youthful days with competition, humor, and mischief. We both absolutely loved sports, primarily football. I loved being the class clown and engaging in playful fights, perhaps fueling my passion for football. Randy and I played for the Calaveras Raiders—he was the quarterback, and I was the tight end. Despite losing more games than winning, those memories remain precious, devoid of any sense of defeat. We still talk about these days to this date. Our teenage years involved the typical antics of boys our age: prank calls, exploration, and a growing desire for independence.

As a child, I learned the value of diligence by growing up with hardworking blue-collar workers as parents. My dad worked at a sawmill and my mom worked at a factory. I'd wake up after they had already started working. When not with Randy, I spent time with my Uncle Dale in the small town of MT Ranch. Here, I learned different life lessons, from the value of hard work to witnessing the pitfalls of drug use. These experiences shaped my understanding of what to embrace and avoid in life.

Upon moving back to Nebraska in the 7th grade, we experienced a challenging period of change. While transitioning through three different junior high schools, I struggled to fit in and frequently resorted to fighting. I also enjoyed fighting so, that part of it did not really bother me compared to not having any friends. It was here I met Jason, my second-best friend, who introduced me to a different world. Our friendship, borne out of necessity in a science project, grew into a strong bond. Jason, a victim of bullying and an exceptional artist, found a protector in me, and I, a loyal friend to him. We were constantly together, one of us always staying the night at his or my house. Jason's interest always leaned towards supernatural and ghosts. His interests became mine, and we would often use his Ouija board. I remember a moment in my basement. Jason, using the board, said, If this is Satan, then give us a sign. Directly after that, the TV went off. Our terror quickly subsided as we realized the station had gone off air.

In eighth grade, my relationship with Melissa, a remarkable woman who would later become my wife. We bonded over shared values and backgrounds—both accustomed to modest living and raised to cherish and defend what we love. Despite challenges, including resistance from her family, our commitment to each other never wavered. Melissa and I were very close during childhood. I knew her deepest secrets, and she knew mine. I never hoped to be apart from her. Melissa was everything to me then. Melissa's upbringing was more challenging than mine. Without going into her childhood, this is one reason she's tough today. She is also very smart in school, always scored A's in her classes. In 8th grade, I signed up for classes to be with her. Surprisingly, we made it to 29 years of marriage.

A large part of my life was sports. My dream was always to play professional football. However, the only chance I had of doing anything professional was bowling. My Dad, who was a semi-professional bowler before my birth, imposed it on me. I had several tournament wins and finished 2nd in the entire state of Nebraska. I could have received college scholarships if I hadn't switched to the adult league before turning 18. Despite my age, I surpassed most adult bowlers. I'll impress the adults by winning money through gambling. The death of my dad also replaced this in '92, and the bond between Melissa and I just grew stronger, and bowling was only a memory at that point.

Despite life throwing curveballs, including job losses and familial conflicts, my resolve only grew stronger. The decision to join the Army was both a necessity and a turning point. It was a means to provide for my new family, despite the sacrifices it entailed. My wife's half-American, half-Korean heritage, and the strong values instilled in me by my upbringing—hard work, loyalty, and honesty—have profoundly shaped my character.

This chapter of my life, replete with lessons and hardships, paints a vivid picture of the foundations that molded me into the person I am today. Even prior to the military, I was a very hard worker. I was not afraid of hard work. I worked as a mechanic for Kmart, I would mow properties with a push mower on the weekends, and I helped contractors with labor on days I was free. Once my father passed away, money was very hard to find. I ended up taking a full-time job scrubbing floors at a grocery store until 7 AM. Then go pick up Melissa for school. This was hard to maintain since I didn't drop out of school. My mother wanted me to graduate highschool. I occasionally napped in class, and my teacher, Mr. Black, was quite helpful, particularly in my first two automotive classes. I don't know his story, but I feel the teacher saw himself in me. His name was Mr. Black, and he is one teacher I hope I never forget. By bringing in cars to work on, I could earn my grade and he would allow me to sleep in between the cars. He knew my story with my dad and needing the money for bills with my mom out of work with back surgery. I think he could relate to my situation from something in his past. Because of sports, I gained enough credits to graduate, and only had one class I had trouble with. Required to do 40 hours of volunteer work for our class, I lacked the resource time. I filled every minute of my life with work. I told the recruiter about my inability to graduate because of this. Luckily, the recruiting station accepts volunteers, and he gladly approved my volunteer paperwork. In retrospect, I possibly outsmarted the school, but I feel I balanced it out with my service.

Chapter 2: The Crucible of Service: From Basic Training to Beyond

In life, certain experiences evoke fear, but often, we don't truly know what should frighten us until we face it. The transformative day of October 4th, 1994, will always be in my memory. It was the last day I spent with my wife before embarking on my journey to basic training, marking the beginning of the longest day I had yet encountered. My initiation into the military was a grueling 40-hour stretch with no sleep, culminating in an unexpected wake-up call during roll call. This was my introduction to what a smoke session entailed—a series of physically taxing exercises meant to test our limits. The training days that followed were a blend of monotonous routines and unexpected challenges, including the last test, known as the Super bowl. One significant lesson was the realization that certain training scenarios, like reacting to incoming fire, didn't quite match the real-world speed and intensity of combat; Even this early, I could feel the bond between veterans. I felt like I was somebody and I was doing something important.

One of our recruits was coming in as a singer for the military. Our Drill SGT made him teach all of us God Bless The U. S. A by Lee Greenwood. Every time we lined up or stood around, singing, it would be required. He was a talented singer, however, the rest of us, not so much. I remember when a general came through our barracks. We all sang it for him, and I can't speak for everyone, but I felt proud of that song.

The sense of being someone helped me get through most of my basic training tests. Becoming a soldier was my utmost desire. Things like the Gas Chamber, where we gained confidence in our gas masks, were a part of training that everyone never forgets. It was unpleasant to exit the chamber with snot and tears caused by the CS gas. We would do a lot of tasks that I did not realize were rewiring my brain. Things that did not seem normal to non-veterans became very normal to us. Things like the Drill SGT asked me, What makes the green grass grow? "Blood! Blood! Blood! Makes the green grass grow", we would respond. All this type of training changes you, and it's very effective. I learned how to use anger to help me get through tough times. During weapons qualification week, we received more of this therapy that changes our thoughts. The targets were always black silhouettes of a person, but I never questioned why. I would later learn why and how close to reality they were. Shooting something resembling the familiar paper target is easier. Anger fuels this as the norm.

Graduation day finally came, and a few hours later, I would start Advanced Individual Training. Despite being primarily infantry, some may pursue specialized training. For me, that was 63S Heavy Wheel Vehicle Mechanic. Advanced training was much easier for me. My career as a mechanic started off well. I also had developed confidence and became a squad leader for our class. Prior to the military, I was unaware of this additional skill. I also feel like by the end of my career, I was an outstanding leader. I feel today that is one of the best characteristics I have.

After completing advanced individual training, I received orders for my first duty station: Korea. I had hoped to avoid this, desiring to stay closer to my wife. In Korea, life revolved around adapting to a new environment and building camaraderie with fellow soldiers. I embraced my role as a mechanic and thrived, gaining rank quickly. My time in Korea also provided an unexpected opportunity to connect with a part of my wife's family heritage. As fate would have it, my duty station was near her mother's hometown. In Korea, the freezing wetness and smell are unforgettable. When you get off the plane, you quickly learn. What you're able to do in Korea is truly based on how close to North Korea you are. We had a few soldiers available for leave. Without a pass, curfew was midnight. I found a loophole to this. My uncle lived in Osan, so I would visit him there. I'll be there until Sunday, then I'll go back.

My next assignment was at Fort Bliss, a transition filled with both anticipation and eventual disappointment. The only joyous outcome from this period was the birth of my son. A lack of camaraderie and a rigid chain of command that lacked empathy marred my experience at Fort Bliss, especially during a family emergency involving the birth of my child. My wife's aunt passed away, and we went back up to Nebraska to be with her family. Her Aunt Judy was an amazing woman. She was the role model in my wife's childhood. My wife was 9 months pregnant. The night preceding the funeral, Melissa went into labor. I drove her to the Air Force base to have the baby. Delivery complications caused my son to have jaundice because of the cord around his neck. The doctors told my wife she would be in the hospital for 3 days. The issue was I had to report back to Ft Bliss in 3 days. Calling my chain of command to inform them. I was told by the 1SG to leave my wife and son at the hospital and return alone. I suggested he call the MPs, because I would go AWOL before I would leave my wife and son in the hospital. The commander approved my leave extension, allowing me to bring my wife and son back with me. Here, I encountered this leadership type. Compelled by my detestation for Ft Bliss, as well as bills and healthcare, I reenlisted as the quickest way to leave this base. I had asked our Platoon Leader to reenlist me. She was one of two people I respected. The platoon leader did not show up, while my wife and I stood with the retention NCO. Just another letdown from this unit. The Battalion XO did the ceremony so I could get reenlisted. Six months later, I would leave for Germany.

When arriving in Germany, there were various challenges to overcome, including healthcare emergencies and housing issues. However, this station marked a turning point in my career. I found myself in a more supportive unit where I could grow as a tactical NCO. Once again, Fort Bliss gave me another gift. After reenlisting, they did not file my reenlistment paperwork. Once I got to Germany, the Army stopped paying me. This went on for a couple of months to get fixed, causing me to almost lose my car and forced us to rely on food pantries for food. The chain of command did everything they could to get it fixed. They even took up a donation to help me get meat. I truly learned what leadership looked like. My aspirations to join the all-army boxing team got put to the test in Germany. Despite an initial setback, I learned valuable lessons about resilience and the importance of individual effort in boxing. I put my focus on my career at this point and started getting ready for the promotion board.

Amidst the looming deployment to Bosnia, I experienced uncertainty and apprehension. Conversations with fellow soldiers who had experienced combat brought home the realities of war. These stories ranged from tragic to bizarre, shaping my expectations for what lay ahead. Despite these looming challenges, I remained the person I had always been—confident, jovial, and deeply committed to my family, country, and brothers-in-arms.

Promotion boards in the Army are pivotal, and my experience was no exception. Despite a nerve-wracking start and a humorous mishap during questioning, I earned my promotion. My time in Germany was a period of personal and professional growth and learning. While I was present, my superiors promoted me to SGT and gave me the opportunity to lead. I received my promotion to E-5 SGT after my deployment to Bosnia.

Chapter 3: From Bosnian Grounds to Nightstalker Bounds

When I left my family for Bosnia, I experienced tension and heightened awareness of the risks in a conflict zone. My journey began with a train ride to Taszar, Hungary, alongside SGT Anderson, a man of few words but an exceptional leader. The initial phase of our deployment started by a series of unfortunate events, including an incident involving a lost pistol and a physical altercation in a tent that resulted in an all-night interrogation. While searching for the pistol, a 1SG struck me upon entering the tent. We spent the next day getting the equipment ready for the 3-day drive to Camp Bedrock, Bosnia.

As we journeyed from Hungary to Camp Bedrock in Bosnia, the scenery transformed dramatically. The gorgeous landscapes of Croatia contrasted with the war-torn buildings of Bosnia, presenting a stark reminder of the harsh realities of conflict. Poverty in Bosnia reached unimaginable levels, forcing people to take desperate measures to survive, unlike in the United States or Germany. As I crossed over the bridge separating Croatia and Bosnia, I saw the leftover signs of war. The first thing I remember was a school that was filled with .50 caliber bullet holes. I saw families burning their yard to stay warm. The impact on Bosnian individuals was unknown to me. They appeared beaten down from the years of fighting.

At Camp Bedrock, my role extended beyond that of a mechanic and wrecker operator. My mission included setting up checkpoints and towing vehicles with incorrect license plates.

These experiences exposed me to the harsh realities of life in a war zone, from children selling their siblings for candy to the consistent danger of land mines. This deployment was a significant shift from my previous experiences, demanding adaptability and resilience. I remember watching the children running around and noticed none of them played in the grass. It seemed they only walked on concrete. They educated the children about land mine risks, depriving them of childhood joys. Bosnian kids were years ahead of US children in understanding life's challenges.

Life at Camp Bedrock was austere, with limited amenities and the PX truck as our only source of shopping. As a soldier, life was a blend of duty, relaxation, jokes, and pranks to break the monotony. One memorable prank involved misleading flyers about boot polishing services, highlighting the lighter side of soldier camaraderie in challenging environments. We also posted signs on April Fools' Day that Lou Ferrigno was coming to talk to everyone. Unaware of the date, people eagerly expected his arrival. The jokes would get us through the times of missing our families.

My responsibilities also included base support. Which sometimes meant recovering vehicles outside the wire. These missions underscored the adaptability and courage inherent in military service. We often ventured into uncertain and dangerous situations. An example is a Humvee falling off a steep cliff. Their salvation relied solely on the axle stuck to the tree stump. I had to pull them out with a winch from the wrecker. Without the tree stump, they would have fallen 100 feet. No injuries occurred on that miraculous day.

Back in Germany, my wife faced challenges of her own. Navigating her pregnancy alone in a foreign country. An incorrect and alarming diagnosis by her doctor added to our worries. Revealing the inconsistencies in military medical care. This experience, coupled with the stresses of deployment, contributed to my growing reluctance to expand our family. I made it home on leave for the birth of my daughter. She was born in Landstuhl, Germany.

During this time, I made the impulsive decision to undergo a vasectomy. A procedure offered by the military to maintain surgeons' skills. The surgery coincided with a heightened security situation following a Taliban attack on a naval ship. This shift meant full battle readiness and longer, more strenuous guard shifts. Which was challenging during my recovery.

As my deployment neared its end, I began preparing for my next assignment with the 160th Special Operations Aviation Regiment (SOAR), also known as the Nightstalkers. The move involved meticulous planning and coordination, reflecting the complexity of military relocations. My integration into this elite unit marked a significant shift in my military career, fostering a renewed sense of purpose and dedication.

The Night Stalker Creed, embodying the ethos of this distinguished unit, became a guiding principle in my life, resonating deeply with my commitment to service and excellence. As I concluded my time in Bosnia and looked forward to the challenges ahead with the Nightstalkers, I carried with me the lessons and experiences of my journey, ready to uphold the standards of one of the most elite units in the military.

Night Stalkers Don't Quit!–a motto that captures the relentless spirit and unwavering commitment of the 160th SOAR, was a creed that I embraced wholeheartedly, marking a new chapter in my military career.

Chapter 4: Beyond the Creed: Becoming a Part of the 160th SOAR

When you join the Night Stalkers, you carry with you the legacy of those who had served before you. This unit had a long, proud reputation. The unit's creed outlines the legacy of being a part of it. The unit was renown for their part in Somalia and the movie Black Hawk Down.

When my family and I arrived at Hunter Army Airfield in Savannah, Georgia in September 2000, we embarked on a new chapter. Initially, I knew little about the 160th Special Operations Aviation Regiment, except for the upcoming challenge of Green Platoon, a rigorous selection course designed to assess and affirm one's commitment.

They held Green Platoon at Fort Campbell, Kentucky. An intense test of physical and mental endurance. It began with a deceptively long run, designed to test our reaction to perceived failure. The days were grueling, marked by constant uniform changes, demanding physical training, and exhaustive classes covering advanced skills like combat lifesaving and map reading. Each day ended with the daunting option to quit, which none of us took.

One memorable challenge was Black Day, infamous among the trainees. It involved a surprise early morning gear inspection. Followed by a punishing physical trial, including a run with telephone poles. While running, the cadre left behind had thrown our gear into a massive pile. We got back and we're told we had 5 minutes to get our gear, change, and get ready for the 6-mile road march. A disorienting six-mile ruck march followed, with mismatched or ill-fitting boots. The accurate test was a mental one, teaching us the crucial lesson of never leaving a comrade behind. Troublesome boots: small or too big. We aimed to bring everyone back within the time limit. Only one of the 4 road marches would cause failure, and you were unaware of which one it was.

The training culminated in a simulated survival and evasion exercise. The unit always used the local sheriff's department to track us with dogs. This exercise cemented the skills and mindset necessary for the operations we would face.

Graduation day marked my official entry into the Night Stalkers. Fulfilling a significant personal goal and deepening my commitment to the elite group's ethos. The day finally comes that I am officially a Night Stalker. I was ready to use the knowledge I received. At this school, I learned to push beyond my limits and seek greater challenges. The school deliberately exposed you to situations designed for failure. Embrace the Night Stalker spirit, adapt and overcome.

The special operations world differs from the conventional army that I was used to. I was now surrounded by type A personalities. The unit is full of people that would rather die than quit. The initial week in the unit sticks in my memory. They told me about this room called the Thunderdome. People solved issues in this room. A disagreement happened between platoon SGT and the specialist in our presence. Their conversation revolved around Thunderdome attendees. I just sat in the room, keeping to myself. I remained uncertain about my behavior. Upon hearing the SGT's words to Santana, I realized he wouldn't leave until he entered the Thunderdome with someone. Unbelievable. This was real. Nobody really knew me very well. Santana looks over at me and said, I will go in with SGT Dunn. My Platoon Sergeant told me, make a point, but don't kill him. My platoon SGT was the only person who knew I had boxed before. Santana appeared with a smudged face and hands clasped in front. The jab caused a quick change in his look, revealing a lack of plans. He threw a slow punch, and I countered with an overhand right. Santana hits the ground like a sack of potatoes and the platoon sergeant quickly puts an end to it.

I quickly learned that the pace of this unit was quick. The creed they held went beyond mere words. They were a way of life. Your work knowledge may change abruptly. I would find myself TDY (temporary duty) all the time. We would be gone, training with some of America's elite of the elite. Working with SEALs, Special Forces, and Rangers was impressive, to say the least. Despite my tactical and proficient training, war seemed unlikely. Everything occurred prior to 9/11. I arrived almost exactly a year to the day of the unit prior to 9-11.

September 11, 2001, all of this ended. I got to work after PT ended. We had a TV upstairs with the news usually on. That day, everyone was surrounding the TV. Silently, we shared a common understanding. We were going to war, and it started on our soil.

Chapter 5: Echoes of Kandahar: Through the Soldier's Eyes

That day forever changed everything we knew. Life's unexpected changes surpassed our expectations. America became united; the soldiers were champing at the bit to deploy, and I was no different. Our meeting with the commander didn't include any mention of our battalion's schedule. He wondered if we had any inquiries. I immediately stood and asked, When do we go next, sir? His simple response stayed with me for years. Watch what you wish for; you might just get it, he said. It wasn't four months later we were gearing up to deploy.

My wife drove me to the "A" dock. This is where we staged prior to leaving. We would begin our trip to Kandahar, Afghanistan. I remember giving her a kiss goodbye. Tears ran down her cheeks. My young children, unable to comprehend the situation. I never enjoyed long goodbyes. I preferred to handle my goodbyes like a band-aid and just rip it off. The longer the goodbye, the more it hurts. I always felt bad leaving, a little uneasy about what was coming. The smell of JP8 from the C5s and C17s' exhaust lingers in my memory. On this day, it was a C5, the largest cargo aircraft in the Air Force Fleet. To give you an idea of how big they are. While training overseas, we played arena football against the crew members of the C-5. The aircraft's nose and back ramp opened, allowing entrance from the back and exit from the front. Once we boarded the giant, we proceeded to the upper deck and comfortably settled into our seats. The seats were facing backward, and this also created an odd feeling in my stomach.

Flight seemed to take forever, first stop in Germany, then Kandahar. We landed early in the morning. When the sun appeared on the horizon. We saw our new home, and I sat down to eat my first meal. I had some smoked oysters, crackers, and cheese in my bag and decided this was breakfast. We sat our bags down, and the workday began. We had much to accomplish prior to their arrival. Tents needed setting up, bathrooms had made, power running. We all started and established the camp. Being in this unit was significantly important. We saw problems as challenges. Building a bathroom was the assigned task for that day. Fortunately, a junkyard was available on the campsite where we discovered an old phone booth. After cutting the back and removing it, we placed a 55-gallon drum underneath. We made a hole and added a toilet seat. Then hung a sign Don't Piss Where You Shit. Understand that to dispose of waste. This had to be burned, but pee doesn't burn easily. We took a 3-inch PVC pipe and dug it in the ground about 3 feet down, leaving the top hanging out about waist high. We would poop, then walk out and pee in the pipe. Upon detecting urine odor, we'd dig a new hole and fill the old one.

The food we ate did not age, like a fine wine. We ate MREs (meal ready to eat.) It comprised a meal. This one time we traded the French a pallet of ours for theirs. We attempted another trade after they left, but they promptly turned us down. One even asked how we ate those; hell, I even wondered that. Between the long days and the lack of food, it was hard to keep up morale. We passed our days when off by playing chess or playing a game of a veteran version of Horse. We called it jackass.

One day we were walking back to camp when a rocket came flying in. With a loud explosion, the rocket entered a solitary generator. We all dove to the ground, trying to get our bearings. Ears were echoing from the loud explosion. Mortars and rockets were picking up more with the warmer weather moving in. Warmer weather didn't just increase fighting, but also brought another threat. The increase in sand vipers and camel spiders and scorpions. Soldiers had additional tasks to handle because of this addition. Several of the other soldiers would catch them in water bottles and boxes. They would make the scorpions and camel spider fight. Killing the boredom was the proper goal. At night, the crew would use their training as the mission tempo intensified. Everyone Joined us by the burn barrel as our unit prays for mission participants.

Foreign military often gathered in Kandahar. We had Canadians, French, and Norwegian in our immediate area of the camp. Every day, the camp grows and becomes more like a military base. The burn pit was near to where we were staying, as well as the area they designated as our range. One night I was asleep when the loudest boom I've ever heard. The vibration almost knocked me out of my cot. When I stepped outside, I couldn't see anything because of a direct hit. The next morning, I heard the details. During the night, a Canadian unit was at the range when one of our aircraft shot at them and killed several of our allies. Once again, the morale left the soldiers. I felt so ashamed. Regardless of my innocence, dishonor lingered. We attended their memorial together. I couldn't make eye contact with anyone. How difficult is it to invite the soldiers who killed your brothers to the memorial? Regrettably, there will be additional memorials. We all gathered at the flight line to say goodbye to two fallen warriors. It's crazy how seeing unfamiliar faces who didn't make it home doesn't make you realize it could've been you on that flight.

Months passed, allowing people to return to Germany briefly. We would leave our weapons and catch a return flight. It was my chance to take a break for a few days. When we tried to return to Kandahar, there were no flights available to Kandahar. The war moved northward, and supplies redirected to Bagram Air Base. To get there, we must fly to Bagram and arrange for helicopter transportation. A flight from Bagram to Kandahar on a Ch-47 is an endless flight. This aircraft was already war baptized. To allow for a return fire, the crew chiefs had already removed the windows. Flight was cold, the crew chiefs were concerned after two hours. We quickly realized a fuel problem, leading to the grounding of the aircraft. We hit the ground hard enough to break the landing gear on the aircraft. I recall gazing out the windows and realizing we were in an unfavorable location. Every area around us I could see was much higher than us. I looked up and saw the other Chinooks flying circles around us. I felt like something was dying, and the vultures were circling above us. Frantically, crew chiefs worked on the aircraft to resume our flight. Time changed and minutes felt like hours to me. All we could do was stand watch, looking for anything moving towards us. The aircraft fired back up with a loud rumble; we lifted off the ground again. Landing back down in Kandahar. Being present made me happy, a first for me. Things could have easily turned out differently.

Shortly after, I returned to the United States. My baptism of war and Afghanistan finally reached an end and I finally get to go back to my wife and kids and see them again. Certain emotions always arose as I returned home. Upon leaving my wife. Finally, boarding the plane meant the workday was over and I could relax.

Chapter 6: The Unseen Battles: Striving for Normalcy Amidst Chaos

The gauntlet of deployments continued with a new land for us to operate in. We moved to Iraq to capture Saddam, taking a large force with us, unlike the team elements we had in Afghanistan. I operated in a classified area, and I cannot reveal its location. We spent hours in the sun, with hours of boredom. After the war, we returned to the states and formed teams in Iraq, beginning in Mosul. We now had personnel in five different theaters. I spent three months each in Iraq, the states, and Afghanistan.

My first rotation to Iraq quickly showed me the differences between Afghanistan and Iraq to fight. The tactics were very different. The number of rockets and mortars increased in Iraq. We had local nationals working on the base with us. We would have to guard them while they did labor jobs, like filling sandbags. You could detect attacks easily. Rockets arrived daily, just like the mortars. I was lying in my bed getting ready to go to sleep one night when a rocket exploded just above my hooch. Had it gone 50 feet further, it would have hit my room. Throughout the night, I lay awake, unable to sleep, my mind aware of the nearness of the end.

The moment I remember was leaving for the states in the morning. I had handed off my weapon to the person relieving me. We took an attack from a small squad element. I grabbed an extra M4 and rounded up the local nationals and put them in a bunker. I had one of my soldiers guard one side of it while I guarded the front. Unsure of locals' alliances in attacks, I guarded against potential rear assaults on the perimeter. I was standing next to the bunker when one local told me he wanted out because he was hot. I let him know I was as well and to please sit. His gaze met mine, prompting me to direct the interpreter to relay my words to him: Better to be alive and warm than dead and cold. He should take a seat. As he sat down, he said he had to pee. The problem is, he was drinking and behaving erratically. I threw him an empty water bottle. The local worker watched and then watched me. He reiterated his need to pee, and I responded by urging him to do so. He got up, but I promptly proposed using a bottle instead. His answer was negative. I clarified you would stay in the bunker. I made it very clear you can piss in the bottle or the bunker, but you're not coming out. Chatter ensued when the other guard shouted about a gun. The interpreter yelled, No, no, no! as I was raising my weapon. Fake! Fake! Fake, he said. He grabbed the gun and showed it to us. It was a cigarette lighter. I almost killed a man over a cigarette lighter.

I ended up rotating back home later that night. I was prepared to go back, indifferent to ever seeing Iraq again. The rotations from now on got blurry. I was not happy, deployed or home. Putting on a fake smile and striving to lead is increasingly challenging. I had earned a reputation for being reliable. I was good at my job and truly did everything I could to get everyone home. My problem is, what I showed on the outside was not how I was feeling inside. Soldiers were looking up at me because of my leadership skills, but inside, I hated myself. Happiness was no longer in me, deployed or home, by this time. Nothing seemed to spark my interest or attention. The absence of motivation made going home uneventful. Driving back to our part of the camp, I was yelling at one of our soldiers. Right as I saw him point and scream. A mortar round hit near our truck. Gravel scattered as I sped up to leave. Another mortar hit a soldier running down the sidewalk. We arrived back at our part of the camp and my soldier went into the building, leaving his gear on. He would not take off his gear. I perceived the soldier uniquely, outwardly displaying my frustration with his refusal to leave the buildings. He then decided he no longer wanted to live and made suicidal intentions. We shared common feelings. Not shareable now. Today, I truly think this is how our war has differed from other wars. Number of times you were over there. We all lacked space to push things down. Sharing these feelings with my family is not something I will do. I believed I safeguarded them, so at home, I felt justified in my actions for them. I didn't realize I was hurting myself simultaneously.

The enchanting smile would come back upon returning home. I was happy to see my family, don't get me wrong, but I sometimes felt like I no longer knew how I was supposed to act around them. Things were bothering me, and my temper was shorter. I did not notice these things, but I know my wife did. When home, I stay busy with car projects or anything to keep my mind occupied. Shortly after, I returned to the deck, and it was time to leave. Going back to Afghanistan.

Chapter 7: In the Shadow of Loss: The Weight of War's Reality

I returned to the place that felt like my second home, Afghanistan. We stationed ourselves permanently in Bagram at that point, and the deployments became repetitive. The tempo never slowed, always faster than in Iraq. The welcome committee was always happy to greet us with some music from rockets and mortars. Nothing out of the ordinary happened during this time frame. I would talk with Marcus Morales and Kip Jacoby. The conversations were always different between the two, but I truly enjoyed both of their company. Marcus was a very experienced warfighter and medic. I trusted him more than most doctors. We would sit outside in front of the hooches and have conversations, mostly kind of philosophical conversations. Because of different shifts, conversations were never lengthy. Kip would talk to me mostly about cars; he and his fiancée were building a car together, and I loved cars, so the conversations would usually be pretty good. Without missions, he would frequent the Motor pool for conversations. It's time for me to go back home. The commander and I planned to rotate back, but sandstorms always caused flight delays. The interesting thing is, prior to us leaving, our flight crews captured our commander and tied him up, and placed him by the flagpole. Since we did not fly, he spent the day getting his revenge. Only person he did not go after was the new forward commander, Maj. Reich. He was a prominent leader, and I still remember having to do the briefs in front of him. Like other officers, he expects me to correct my slides for grammar and more. I knew he was just making me do better, but it would be frustrating. We ended up flying out that night and headed back home. It was not until our return that I discovered the commander's intentions for Maj Reich.

We got back, and LTC Tierney asked the motor pool guys to take Maj Reich's tires off his jeep. Guys strung toilet paper all over his jeep and put it up on blocks. Everyone knew how much he loved his jeep.

June 28th, 2005, about ten days after we got home, the reality of our job hit home. I came to work and shortly after. They were infilling 8 Seals to rescue 4 other seals that were fighting for their life. Upon entry, a soldier on a cliff fired an RPG, hitting the Chinook's fuel tank. It was the biggest American casualty during that war. Sixteen men lost their life on the aircraft, and 3 lost their life fighting on the mountain. If this story sounds familiar, it's because they made a movie about it called Lone Survivor. The mission participants wouldn't return, unlike the movie. A sudden sense of sadness and disbelief. I volunteered to help with the funerals. The team I belonged to handled three funerals. It was challenging for everyone in the unit, not just me. We had lost no one in our unit.

After the funerals were over, I remember going with several other soldiers to help Marcus's wife pack up their house. She was moving in with her family if my memory serves me. Looking at Marcus's young children, wondering if they understood their dad would no longer be coming back. The 160th and the Ranger Battalion will acknowledge the bravery of their father. A horrible feeling that one day someone would help my family pack up the house. I never could really shake this feeling, and it bothered me a lot. Things were going further down for me. I no longer wanted deployment in my heart, even though I never tried to avoid it. I never informed them; deployments became routine. When I left, my wife had stopped crying and seemed to think nothing was too terrible because I didn't discuss it. Internally was a distinct feeling. I was feeling like me and my family were not that close anymore. I think, to be honest, I was pushing them away without even realizing it. Subconsciously, maybe I was trying to make it easier on them when my turn came up. My wife not sleeping in the same bed made me feel distant.

I returned to Iraq this time. My discomfort in Iraq remains unexplained. It was such a different type of war. I remember seeing from the base a very large puff of smoke in the air. Hearing a tremendous boom, I assumed it was a rocket or mortar. Turns out a VBIED (Vehicle-Borne Improvised Explosive Device) positioned in front of a police station. When our MPs and local first responders showed up, they detonated two more in the same traffic circle, killing and injuring lots of people. Each day of the deployment felt explosive. We had a US Contractor coming to our base to help us work on an up-armored Mercedes that we found in a junkyard. I got it running. I had gone to the front gate that morning to meet him and take him to our area. From my position, I could see people walking on. Suddenly, a loud explosion goes off. Individuals concealed themselves, a few behind sandbags, as others vocalized distress. A vehicle that was between the outer perimeter and our perimeter had run out of gas. Guards approached the car to inquire about the situation. The female Iraqi driver then detonated an IED, resulting in the death of herself and her estimated 13-year-old daughter. Some debris from the explosion hit the contractor and broke his leg. Brief ringing in my ears, another situation that always makes me wonder how I made it through. All deployments have become indistinguishable. To this day, remembering where events occurred remains challenging and requires significant contemplation. I know I was happy about going home from this deployment. This marked my last presence in Iraq on the 160th.

Chapter 8: The Crossroads of Service: Reflections on Duty and Departure

I did several more deployments to Afghanistan on the 160th. My attitude and personal life were showing the tolls. I lacked joy in my actions and lost interest in the military. Post-deployments, I had seen enough and lacked clarity on desires. A new vice took hold, and I started playing poker. I find peace in focusing on poker math and learning the game. Submerging myself in the game. I spent all my time playing and studying until my tired brain could sleep thoughtlessly. A bothersome thought kept running in my mind. Upon arriving home from work, I would promptly begin playing on the computer. It never even occurred to me I was pushing my family away even more. Sometimes, I'd start using the computer at 6 pm after coming home, finishing just before leaving for work at 4 am. By this time, I got promoted to Staff Sergeant and was supposed to attend BNOC (Basic Noncommissioned Officers Course). Leaving the military was my goal in order to manage my emotions.

The day of reckoning has come. I went to BNOC and returned to the unit in less than a month. I had failed the APFT, and this just continued my downward spiral. The unit was becoming more difficult. No one will volunteer for our unit's new battalion in Washington state. The unit went to the regular army, requesting their help in filling vacancies. For that to occur, my unit had to open their records and let the Department of the Army assess our personnel numbers and occupied positions. We had to request the longest-serving individuals to depart when every position was occupied. Around this time, our company gained a new 1SG, which was unfortunate for me. He was someone I strongly disliked and considered an inadequate leader. I may have been empty inside and pushed my family away by this point, but the one thing I never lost up to this day was my love for my fellow soldiers. I took my responsibility as an NCO seriously and at no time did I ever put my personal safety ahead of the safety of my soldiers. Our 1SG was not that NCO. He reciprocated my hatred for him as well. To give you an idea, one thing he did that I truly did not like was he put the evaluations for the NCOs in a file and gave the lower enlisted soldiers access to read our evaluations. Never demean a fellow NCO in front of lower enlisted, which was exactly what he did.

The biggest issue he had with me was the fact that I failed BNOC. He would continuously spread the word about my failure and inadequate leadership. The day came for my evaluation to be due, and my direct supervisor, a SFC whom I had a lot of respect for, wrote it. He was tough, but fair, and shared his deep passion for the wellbeing of his soldiers. He turned in my eval to the 1SG, who instantly called him back to see him. My 1SG wanted him to change my evaluation to needs improvement because of me failing the PT test. Let me pause for a second and explain something. While in the Army, the instructors evaluate you during your time at a leadership course. The instructors give you the rating at the conclusion of the course. Your Unit only rates you for the rest of the year. My time spent at the school is called non-rated time, because you already got rated by the school. It still goes in your file as an evaluation; it is just not written by your chain of command. The 1SG wanted to ensure no chance of my promotion by giving me another critical evaluation. Apart from the PT test, I never struggled with anything in the Army. My Platoon SGT refused and instructed the 1SG to write the change request, otherwise he would escalate the matter to the Sergeant Major.

Despite this, 1SG persisted and summoned me and my platoon SGT to convince me. I required a negative evaluation. He told me I should agree to it because it's not fair for other NCOs to be graded similarly to me since I had failed a school. I told him I did not agree, and he then started saying the question again. I then answered him again. He then repeated for a third time. I then told him I had answered his fucking question and if he asked it again, I would come across his desk to answer him. After pulling me out, my Platoon SGT closed the door behind him. Here is where my temper had gotten.

Continuing forward in time, I returned to BNOC for a second visit approximately four months later. I passed it and returned. I quickly received orders for Korea. The news didn't upset me initially, but then I found out my orders were being deleted. I went in and talked to our command Sergeant Major. I knew him since he was a SFC, and he was another leader I had a lot of respect for. As soon as I walked into his office, he looked at me and said don't worry; I am getting your orders deleted. He didn't want me to leave because of my abilities as a soldier and mechanic. I looked at him and told him; no, I don't want to stay; It is time for me to go. He stood, shut the door, and asked me, You want to go? I nodded yes. Staying means no fair chance with the 1SG around. I detailed his daily belittlement in front of everyone. His gaze met mine as he said, No one has ever requested to leave. We agreed to my departure, and I agreed.

We ended up having an organizational day, which we call those Mandatory fun days. You had to be there, but we promise you'll enjoy it. I encountered the Regimental SGM during my visit. SSG Dunn, what do you think of the duty station I got you? He said. Korea is good, SGM; I have been there before. I said. He said, Yeah, Korea, and chuckled. After pausing, he said, are you serious? Yes, SGM. SGM Said, Check your file tomorrow and let me know if it still says Korea. I didn't want to bring up questions, as I wasn't sure if he was angry at me for failing the PT test or if there was something else happening.

Next day, I checked my file like he told me to do, and the orders told a different story, to Doha, Qatar. I did not know what this was. I quickly learned that it was not a bad thing, as I thought. My only hesitation was with deployment. At first glance, I found myself transported back to the Middle East, confirming my initial thoughts. No uniform required. You did not get issued any gear and only fired my rifle one time to qualify. This was absolutely amazing. I also quickly learned that the base Command Sergeant Major was my old 1SG from Germany. He was another very hard NCO but very fair and cared about his soldiers.

I won't elaborate on Qatar, as there isn't anything noteworthy to mention. Being the first to deploy from Qatar was solely responsible for my luck. The one thing I no longer wanted. We deployed to Kandahar, a place I knew intimately. Base commander wanted me to join them, considering my time in

Special Operations. He knew where I came from because he was my 1SG when I volunteered. The deployment wasn't lengthy. I stayed there for approximately 45 days. Babysitting is what it truly felt like. I returned to Qatar, then later moved to Fort Stewart, where my wife and kids were. This time brought mixed emotions, as it marked my future retirement location. However, I also knew I would deploy again. I made sure not to revisit the 160th and re-board the train. I got assigned to B Co 702nd Forward Support Battalion. The unit was short, and the warrant officer instantly quizzed me. Several days later, he approached me and declared, You shall be the motor sergeant. I naively believed that my military-related problems would vanish once I departed.

Chapter 9: From Ramadi to Retirement: Battles Within and Beyond

Family and I going back to Georgia. knowing shortly after getting there, they are training up for a deployment to Iraq. My only option is to hope that this will be my last army deployment. I saw things as we trained up that I did not like, one being how late they waited to train the support element MOS to run as gun trucks. I was not as concerned with our potential risk prior to me leaving. We were going to be at Al Asad Airbase. It's one of the largest bases there. Base's size prevents most rockets and mortars from hitting inside. When I left, my wife didn't come with me to the airbase. She gave me a kiss and uttered, See you in a year.

Sitting on the C17 leaving was not an unfamiliar experience for me. Excitement filled some younger soldiers, but not me. I was going to the Middle East, but thinking about the return flight. I only hoped to complete this. Arriving at Al Asad Airbase, I quickly learned that what I thought was happening was not the case. We found out that we had to provide a minor element in Ramadi, Iraq, and I will run it. Ramadi was nothing like Al Asad. Ramadi was a minor post bordered by an Iraqi base next to us. In the heart of Ramadi, the base had scattered buildings at the compound's rear. Back gate, watchers on buildings, armed with AK-47s.

Setting up in Ramadi, I found out how bad it really was. No building for us to work in. I had two missions. One was to provide base maintenance support and convoy maintenance support. We were the halfway point for our major supply routes. Convoys halt for repairs and vehicle inspections en route. To train the Iraqi military in Fallujah, we had the second mission, which required going there three times weekly for logistics and maintenance. Risky trips, sometimes without escorts. We often saw IEDs on routes, especially in Ramadi.

I would sit out in front of my room listening to the Iraqi base getting hit. You would hear the sounds of the .50 cal going off in the background. One difficult aspect was the lack of someone to complain or vent to. As the senior person, I constantly prioritized troop morale. I got to where I would try to stay alone in my room. The upcoming chapters will discuss the damage and its implications, which I didn't fully expect. Besides the emotional issues, there were issues with my neck and knees. The neck pain I had was fueling the depression I was feeling. I've lost mobility in my neck as years have passed. It truly is odd how the things that feel normal to you turn out to not be the healthy choice for your mental health. I hardly contacted home anymore and quit doing PT.

Convoys were a regular occurrence, and we encountered a few IED incidents. I always found traveling through Iraqi Police checkpoints to be the worst part because they commonly had IEDs planted next to them. I was in a 10-ton wrecker one convoy when an IED went off and hit the windshield of a couple of vehicles ahead of me. A loud explosion caught everyone's attention. I quickly started scanning the area for a second attack. If it were Afghanistan, you could have expected it to happen. We all made it back with no major injuries. Hated days in bed, asking myself how I've made it this long.

After nearly a year, we returned to the states, hoping this would be our last deployment. After my return, I moved to another company after getting back and was now part of Eco 3-15 infantry. I would take over the motor pool for my 1SG.

Not realizing things were off with me. I know now, but I felt comfortable. I would come home from work and join my family for dinner. Once dinner ended, then immediately retreat to the bedroom. I felt relaxed in the bedroom. Out with family, I felt misplaced. I was starting to really feel like my family was better off without me. My temper was making everyone walk on eggshells. Going to work wouldn't bring me happiness. The problem was I was being beaten up daily by myself.

I stayed because my family needed retirement benefits. I experienced a conflict between my overwhelming desire to not be around and my rational side. Occasionally, I contemplated the most effective method.

The way my life was going now. Fast forwarding to the last few months of my military career. I finally made it to the end of my military career and was about to retire. I thought this was what I wanted. Another sign I should have seen. My lack of self-love made it impossible for me to find happiness in anything. There was only one emotion for me to deal with the next problem. During my military out processing, I had an argument with a VA representative at Fort Stewart. The reason I lost my temper really is not the important thing. What mattered was I still could not control my emotions. To top it off, I also did not file my VA disability because I was mad at one person. Ending my military career with 68 months of my life spent deployed between

Bosnia, Iraq, and Afghanistan. Spent 20 years in the military and over 5 years deployed. It equals over 25% of my military career fighting in foreign lands and now could not figure out what was wrong with me. Truly, I only had one plan, and it wasn't in a career. Planning for both family care and ending my life is my priority. I started calculating how much my family would need without me. I started looking through insurance policies and suicide clauses. Until the end of base, I had uncertainty about actions and life insurance finances.

Leaving the military was a change that everyone thinks they are ready for. The military can rely on me. In the military, I had a purpose. I walk out that gate, and I become nobody. Being unemployed and purposeless, I had to find a lasting solution to support my family.

Chapter 10: Echoes and Asphalt: Navigating Life After Service

To add to my list of critical decisions, I opened up a business. I did this for two reasons: social challenges and job hunting. A person I knew helped me open up the company. I thought this was the perfect idea. I refrained from interacting with people and was mostly solitary. So I got my CDL, bought a truck, and started hauling bulk chemicals. I lacked knowledge about my actions and the situation. I would spend 4 to 6 weeks on the road, driving 11 hours a day, spending 10 hours in a sleeper the size of 63 inches. At first, I started out feeling like I was somebody again. During my travel, things were good. Me doing this did not stop the fighting at home or the distance in our relationship. Despite being in the same room, I felt distant from my family.

One thing I know, I was a great truck driver; The role was a perfect fit and tried to continue to hide my depression and issues I was having from others. I would sometimes drive with no sleep at all. I would lie in bed, and my mind would be constantly running. No matter what I did, I could not sleep. I would then rise and embark on an 11-hour drive, contemplating deeply. It was my desire and brought me happiness in a way. My mindset wasn't conducive to being an entrepreneur. My moods were at both ends of the spectrum multiple times a day. The other problem was I would make very impulsive decisions based on my current mood. I felt blocked in and very distant from everyone. I would avoid people every chance I could. If I went to a restaurant to eat, I would wear headphones so nobody would talk to me. I got angrier over little things. I misconstrued my family's comments to reinforce my feeling of being unwelcome.

I also completed another goal. I couldn't decide how to stop the fight, anger, memories of the lost, and constant solitude. By now, the voice had become even louder, constantly reminding me of my failure. It would tell me how much of a disappointment I was afraid of deploying. Knowing people who committed suicide, that voice highlighted their bravery, while I dwelled on my fears. It did not matter that I never refused a deployment, or that I spent 68 months in these shit holes.

Things at home continued to just decline. My son had gone down the wrong road. He had now started doing drugs and hanging with the wrong people. I held a lot of resentment toward him because I gave him my college benefits from the military, and he failed out the first semester. He lost any chance for scholarships from cross country and quit doing martial arts after winning two world titles while in high school. I thought he wasted life. Instead of helping positively, I worsened things by turning everything into a fight. The anxiety would just keep growing in me. I didn't realize it was anxiety, but I'd have days when I'd wake up feeling off. I would have this deep feeling internally that things were not okay. Days like this would usually be bad days for me. As the feeling continued, my anger would grow. It's like a fire slowly growing inside me, ready to rage. I would grow angrier with everyone and isolate myself even more. Homecoming days pose a challenge for my family and me. It would always turn into a fight somehow. It seemed like the sole solution to erase the feeling. The lack of knowledge about these feelings within my family led to exacerbated issues. Usually, it results in a fight with my son. Today, I feel this was because of my self-hatred and his resemblance to me.

Getting tattoos seemed like another helpful option. I am not sure why, but the pain of getting them done would help. It was like at least feeling the pain was like I could finally feel something besides anger. I would reserve the shop for 8 hr sessions. During those eight hours, I would lie there and allow them to work on me. Don't get it wrong; I do like the ink I have. I have always liked tattoos since I first came into the military. The completion of the work shifted my perspective. Days I would get ink work done would usually follow better days. I can't explain it, but this seemed to be the case. Regrettably, the expensive therapy didn't provide excellent help. I had filled myself with temporary fixes instead of addressing the real problem. At that point, I refused to admit any problems I had. Nighttime drinking helped me sleep. I refrained from drinking and driving while out on the road. I would drink on the road when I was doing my 36-hour reset. My parking lasted for two days. Usually, I discovered that by the time I could start doing the reset, the amount of thinking I was doing mentally exhausted me.

Veterans often express hatred of fireworks because of the noise. This wasn't a big problem for me. I was asleep in my truck and sleeping. I was in a small truck stop parking lot when I heard the noise. Half asleep, I sat in the truck's driver's seat, peering out the window. I realized in my mind. The fire that occurred was solely from fireworks. I attempted to return to sleep and even chuckled at myself. Noises didn't bother me if I expected them. Dead animals and garbage were my biggest brothers on the road. I would never run over those items for fear that they were an IED. This issue persists in my present. I remember one time I was driving a friend of mine home, and a decent-sized box was in the middle of the lane. I don't know why, but I remember stopping and staring at the box. It was not for very long when I realized I was doing it. I genuinely sensed an issue with this box. Just a few issues to address. My ability to see past the anger also gave me a deep-rooted hatred for people from the Middle East. what part they were from made no difference to me. I would find myself in truck stops, see a person wearing a turban, and I could just feel the hatred in me as I would stare at them. I know the source and understand a deep feeling, which we will explore later. Feelings build up from seeing too much horrible stuff. Someone shot a friend of mine point-blank in the Afghan army while guarding an area where the sheik and a company commander met. During the meeting, the Afghan army pulled his pistol and shot my friend point-blank and ran off. I know these types of stories are not uncommon. We would have vehicles hit literally yards from police checkpoints. Is it possible for someone to hide an IED on a road undetected in front of a police checkpoint? Those were the enemies we'd fight there. People that you could not see. These beliefs involve PTSD and depression remarkably. Erroneous yet logical beliefs live in your mind. Let's look at that last example. I had two situations where I lost friends from direct fire. This comprised nine people killed in action by two enemy combatants. In my mind, all Middle Eastern people were enemies who despised Americans. My mind conjured hatred and anger for survival.

Let's pause and reflect on my emotions. I had destroyed my sense of confidence by letting myself tell myself that I was a disgrace to the country because I was afraid of leaving my family unprepared. I continued to tell myself that my kids hated me and my wife hated me. Fear of her seeing others weakened my self-confidence as a man, warrior, and patriot. I was dealing with guilt that some of my friends died, even though there is no direct correlation with them dying because I rotated back home. I did not leave early, nor did I ask to go home; it was just my time. Knowing that I was part of the Dart team and no longer being there also made me feel bad. Being in a DART team didn't directly lead to saving anyone, so there's no reason for it. Fast rotations prevented proper grieving, leading to certain feelings. Shortly after the funerals, I flew back to the sandbox. I buried and pushed back my emotions, ignoring the dangerous nature of our job. No different from a storage unit, your body can only hide a certain amount as well before you leak them out.

Another problem with me at the moment was the spontaneous and impulsive decision-making. Let me give you a few examples of this. I had always wanted a diesel pickup. Finally got my opportunity to do so. I purchased a truck that I absolutely loved. At this point in my life, I owned a semi and a diesel pickup. I would leave and come home several weeks later, and my truck would be full of garbage from my son using it, and usually, something was wrong with it. Of course, I would instantly blame him for what had happened to it. Its age, over 10 years old, is not the important factor. This cycle happened all the time until one day I traded the truck for 95 Camaro based on an irrational emotion. Anger fueled almost every similar situation.

Before everything happened, I bought my son a '78 Z28. We planned to restore it together when he turned 15, so he could have it at 16. Over time, I gained parts for it through trading and buying. I even traded a Nolan Ryan rookie baseball card that was my pride and possession from collecting. One day, I decided my son had disrespected me for no reason and wanted nothing to do with me; I was getting rid of all the parts that I had bought. That is exactly what I did, and I did it for free. I reached out to familiar scrappers, who retrieved my tools, parts, and workbench. Thus, I resolved to cease my labor. My actions only resulted in wasting money, hurting my son, and making things worse for me. These types of things became a normal part of dealing with me anymore.

The next spontaneous decision I made was to replace my old semi with a new truck. I spent 160k dollars with payments of $647.00 a week on a brand-new long-nose Peterbilt 389. Despite its amazingness, I didn't need this truck. Even with this, I still wasn't happy after getting it. Upgrading my truck still did not feel like I accomplished anything by getting it. I accomplished one thing though, and that was throwing us further into debt.

I explain the common actions of veterans with PTSD. I often wonder if sharing with family could make things better. My life should teach others the importance of seeking early help. Despite everything, I remained unaware of the problem in my life.

By the way, I purchased an APU for my truck, costing an additional $13k. This was basically a generator for my truck, so I had power and air conditioning in the truck. A surprising turn of events unfolded, catching me off guard. I woke up shortly after getting it one day and laid there and felt at peace. In Afghanistan, the sound of the generator brought peace, signifying that things were fine and I wouldn't have to spend hours fixing the camp. Minutes passed as I lay there, only then realizing I was in my truck, not Afghanistan. Subsequently, the rush of depression and anxiety returned. I slept better in the truck after getting the APU versus before.

With time on the road, I grew to hate everything, including myself. Being alive, I despised the government and people. In times of distress, I would delay the days to reach home. I just had truly become hollow inside. The other problem was that not being able to keep myself busy nonstop, I drove for eleven hours listening to all the hatred in the news and politics. The world appeared conspiratorial to me.

Despite some ongoing challenges, I would leave and join another company over minor issues. I left the company I currently leased to and went to another company. In under 30 days, I quit and rejoined my old company. I did not care about the money that it cost to make these moves. Avoiding actual problems, still seeking happiness. During nights, I would lie in bed, tears streaming down, fearing my wife's hatred and infidelity. Jealousy consumed me without cause, as I lost all confidence in myself. I think deep down I knew how I was treating everyone and felt like my wife wanted to leave me.

Chapter 11: Beyond the Battle: A Soldier's Struggle with the Aftermath

Living in Georgia, it was not uncommon for hurricanes to come in and either miss us or glance at us. I checked the weather, hoping it would stay clear, so I wouldn't have to leave. This time, the hurricane coming in looked pretty nasty. I rushed home to prepare, feeling increasing anxiety along the way. Every call resulted in more people staying at my house. I went home to my cousin, my brother, my wife, my son, his girlfriend, her sister, and her mom in my house to ride the storm out. When the storm hit the outside, I was feeling the storm inside me. It was impossible to breathe, and the storm unexpectedly lasted longer. Two days later, curfew confined us indoors with fallen power lines. I tried walking and felt on the verge of exploding. Returning home, I learned my son planned to leave, upsetting my wife because of curfew. The demons got ahold of me and blanked out and lost my temper; I remember screaming at him and calling him names. My intention was to provoke a fight. In a fleeting moment, my wife ended it, and I acknowledged that I've shattered my family. I had failed as a father, a husband, and most importantly, I had failed myself.

My son left and seldom came back. It is obvious I had to get help. I could not swallow my pride and go to the VA. Reaching out to another veteran that I knew who was seeing a psychologist led me to the start of getting the help I needed. The next step was to set up an appointment and push myself to attend. I didn't know how the process worked. My understanding is based on what I've seen on TV. Was I supposed to lie down on the couch and get quizzed about how my problem is that I hate my mom? What I experienced was nothing like that. Truthfully, I was unsure of my intentions for going. I believe it's true that the sun shines brightest after a storm.

I went to the appointment, but the discussions did not meet my expectations. The doctor examined my DD214 and, upon seeing my service in the 160th and multiple deployments, he leaned back and shared his expertise in PTSD. Our conversation revolved around his choice to attend SEAL training, driven by curiosity about the special operations community and their mindset. The in person research was for the books he had written on PTSD and helped Fort Stewart use new techniques when dealing with PTSD. He trained multiple therapists in the process to help individuals with PTSD. He asked me about my service and shared his opinion on the frequency of deployments being potentially illegal. During our conversation, he blurted 3 random words. He told me, Just remember those words; we will talk about them later, and he repeated what they were. We continued our conversation and touched on some things that were bothering me inside. Instead of pushing, he seemed to dance around the subjects. He questioned me about his words, but I could only remember two and said them in the wrong order. He asked me if anyone had tested me for TBI. I told him no, and he began talking about symptoms of PTSD and TBI. I really felt like he was talking about me. Some problems I had noticed were right in front of me. It's important that you to realize, at this point in my life, I still have filed no disability claims. I was dealing with memory loss, mainly long-term. I was dealing with anger issues, depression, mood swings, anxiety, spontaneous decision-making. This list just goes on.

He prescribed me medications, and I started taking them; the only drug he prescribed me I would not take was Xanax. I would tell the pharmacy not to fill them. Another issue was my lack of soundness of mind. I couldn't trust others, unable to think independently. Another problem was affecting me. Noticing that my proficiency in math, which was once a strength, was diminishing. The worse part was I was even having issues remembering things about my kids when they were younger. Struggling to recall specific details from deployments, locations, and dates made things difficult. After taking the meds, improvement followed upon finding the correct ones. I don't want to mislead anyone; the right meds did not happen overnight; it was a process. Even my wife noticed a difference. I was more clear-headed; the anxiety had decreased. The other problem is I could then see the financial problems I have caused my family.

I made more mistakes, a path many people follow. The medication was making me feeling better, and feeling better meant I am better. I followed the medication instructions, but I didn't realize my issue wasn't a common cold. You didn't take medicine only after symptoms disappeared. I was grateful for being able to function without being heavily drugged. I wasn't overly happy, nor did I experience extreme lows. Was in the middle. I no longer had the super highs or the super lows. That was exactly what I needed. It lasted for approximately eighteen months. Receiving confirmation of the diagnosis that I already knew, I went to the Veterans Affairs during that time. I then filed the rest of my claims as well. It felt like I was finally getting my life together. I started tackling some of my financial problems.

Just as I believed things were right, surprising news greeted me during my visit to the psychologist. The moment I walked in, everything seemed different. Dr. D met me at the reception counter with a file. After informing me he was closing his practice, he provided me with a 90-day prescription of my meds. He had taken a contract to assist with the PTSD at the local Air Force base. He also gave me recommendations for another psychologist. Once home, I pondered the necessity of enduring it once more. Having to recount my story and uncover the suppressed effects of my medication. It was a choice I didn't desire. I still took the meds that I had and filled the prescriptions that he gave me. My genius plan was, I would slowly stop taking the medication and decided I would keep them with me, and if I needed them, I could take them. This is a flawed common practice. I was unaware of how antidepressants work or their effectiveness. I would take my meds on and off, and my problems slowly started coming back.

COVID had hit, and shortly after I quit taking my meds, I ended up leaving the company that I was with him again and went to another company. This time I started pulling flatbeds and spent more money. As my luck had it, I drove for them for about 7 or 8 months before the early signs of COVID had hit. My lack of experience in the trucking business made it difficult to foresee the impact of economics on the industry. I watched the rates drop, and my expenses going up. Having to go through Des Moines, Iowa, about every few months to help my mom. She was getting older and needed the help. She lived in a small home by herself. Difficulty and low pay hindered the transportation of loads with a flatbed out of Iowa. Trying to keep my mental health together, dealing with the stress of owning a business, made life very hard. The deeper we went into the COVID issues, the harder it got to cover my expenses. We picked up a load and traveled several hundred miles, only to receive a phone call canceling the delivery because of the receiver closing because of COVID. In the event of returning the load to the customer, we would lose all subsequent bookings. One occurrence in a week left me financially strained. I started having truck issues. More unwanted financial issues. The issues I was having only got magnified in COVID. When on the road, it reached a point. Bathrooms became porta Johns, and people began treating us like bottom-class citizens. Without medication, my anger resurfaced after a long time.

With the pattern resurfacing, managing my anger once again proved challenging. To give you an idea of the situation, I remember one day I was getting fuel and was stuck behind the truck in front of the pump and a truck behind me. The driver was in front of me, eating a burger. I got out of the truck and walked over, yanked his door open. I almost pulled him out of his truck for parking in front of the fuel line. The stress of running behind and needing the money complicated with not being able to control my emotions. It happened quickly and with no second thoughts. The fact was, I needed some help, and I knew it. I attempted to visit the doctor that doctor D suggested and set up an appointment. I refrained from going, lacking the resolve.

It didn't take long for the depression to grip me again. I was watching my mother's health fail; my business was failing even faster. I neared rock bottom, but action was necessary. Knowing I had to handle it, I picked myself up and solved the problem. I still had medications prescribed by the doctor. I resumed medication and made life decisions that required me to face. It was impossible to run a business. Years ago, during my PTSD evaluation by a Veterans Affairs doctor, someone made an ironic comment. Her opinion is that most individuals cannot function adequately in a business setting. If she only knew she was correct.

I have developed a saying that seems to be true for the veteran community. Our refusal to quit caused us to reach incredible lows. I picture a soldier digging a hole with his E-Tool. Someone comes up to him and said, I don't think you can dig any deeper. The soldier replies, "Hold my beer," and digs even deeper. He digs to where his hands hurt. With his eyes no longer able to stay open, he noticed that his little shovel had worn out. One day the shovel breaks, and he can no longer dig anymore. It's only that specific time. His sole option is to climb out of the hole or meet his demise. I reached that point and started climbing out of the hole when the sides fell down and hit the bottom hard again. I struggled because of the absence of a plan and strategy to climb the hole's walls. It was time for me to stop and plan instead of simply climbing. This situation affects the veteran community because they do not provide us with the proper tools for this environment. Our emotions during deployment won't function in civilian society.

Chapter 12: Broadcasting Resilience: A Soldier's Journey to Healing Through the Airwaves

With my business completed, my focus shifted to survival and rebuilding my life. My options were simple. Sell my truck and start looking for a job. My lack of civilian job experience left me unsure. In need of guidance, I turned to my daughter for help with my resume. Sitting down and listing my skills was the hardest thing I had done in a while, considering my self-hatred and lack of belief. I checked all the obvious places, like the internet and job listings. It wasn't just about needing a job; the problem was more complex. I needed a job that could afford to take care of two households.

With me closing my business, I could not go back to Des Moines to help her. Comparing her medical benefits to what she would receive if she moved to Georgia, we analyzed the options. Her income would prevent her from making that move. Neither of us could afford the additional costs. One day I got a message from my old 1SG. I asked on Facebook for job posting site recommendations. He contacted me and inquired about my job search. I told him yes, that I had to close my business. I explained the situation to my mom. He was looking for a production supervisor at the place he worked. Without wasting time, I submitted the application. I had two available positions for interviews to help with my situation. I drove back to Des Moines and interviewed for both jobs.

Despite Des Moines not being suitable, I received a call the next day from the other position, which offered more than expected. It's time to plan on moving my mom to Rolla, Missouri, and moving myself without my family. Renting a house in Rolla for me and my mom, and started working as a supervisor for a mining company. I had a few meds left from my previous doctor visits and they were running out. I had to see a doctor again, so I joined the VA.

While spending time with my old 1SG, I realized how much I enjoyed being around him. The problem is that it brought alcohol back into my life. I drank a lot and being irresponsible. The problems were just masked between medication and alcohol.

My buddy and I got involved with the VFW (Veterans of Foreign Wars). I quickly realized this group wasn't suitable for us. Their help for veterans was insignificant, and that's why we went. We spent most of our time working with his project called Salvaje Army. It was a small clothing line that he wanted to create. This grew into reaching out to other soldiers and highlighting the success they had. Playing with firearms and shooting at the range would occupy our time. We both share a passion for firearms. We spent a lot of time shooting and reloading ammo. Although I enjoyed what we were doing, a sense of emptiness persisted. I was helping my mom, away from family, and not making progress on my priorities. One day I looked at him and told him, Why don't we start a podcast? He kind of laughed and asked what we would call it. Laughing was inevitable. Two Drunk Dudes in a Gun Room popped into my mind. Surprisingly, this turned out wonderful. I was also trying to help him get his firearm business off the ground at the same time. Although I declined owning another business, I am still open to providing help. I learned hydrographic methods on my own, which could be an additional contribution he could make. He started doing Cerakoting, and things were starting positively to help veterans. By then, the VA was attending to me and I had restarted my medication. They made some changes from the previous doctor, and initially, I lacked confidence in its effectiveness. This is still one issue I have with trust. I do not have a wide circle of people that I involve myself with. Quickly trusting veterans more than civilians, I am cautious with unfamiliar people. These are things I worked with the VA on during therapy. I could not do it. I did not feel ready to work towards healing. To be fair, I really didn't know what I needed. While on medications, I believed everything was fine. Avoiding confrontation was my intention for now. I think I was still not ready to be honest with myself.

The podcast was exploding, and on Fridays, we do a Facebook live. This really comprised getting drunk and making people laugh. My buddy really loved these days, and I did not so much. Despite my uncertainty, I sensed a shift happening. While continuing to podcast, we had several veterans on our show, and I listened to their amazing stories and some nonprofits. Being with like-minded people felt good. I had a team and felt a sense of belonging, unlike my empty life without one.

My buddy surprised me one day by saying we would record an episode without revealing the topic. I told him, let's do it.

Every year, during a challenging period, my buddy would go on vacation. June always brings back memories of Turbine 33. The plan was to feature it in an upcoming episode. I was alone and felt nervous about doing it. There was uncertainty about the outcome, and honestly, it's our least-watched episode. I was unaware of the profound impact this episode had on my recovery. My buddy's episode was the cause. When the episode ended, I was crying and a complete mess. After recording the episode, I required alone time to contemplate the impact it had. I've never re-listened, but it's ingrained as the change. I had realized that podcasting had turned out to be my therapy. My belief in these remains steadfast. While season one continued, I hoped to podcast as much as possible. The stories from the guests were getting deeper, and my drinking was getting less and less. I no longer wanted to be drunk when I was doing it.

Season one was coming closer to finishing, and I was healing; however, it was not the same for my buddy. He was having a hard time with it. His primary care physician took him off the medications and was over 30 days before the VA could get him an appointment. The problem was her decision to lower his medication dosage. Having gone through withdrawals from the medication, he was in a difficult situation. I tried to be as supportive as I could, but felt helpless; nothing I could do would change what was happening. Unable to help himself, he couldn't help others either. Not I agreed everything upon. He dropped off at the end of season 1. We are not as close as we are anymore. He sought a perpetual drinking partner, but I no longer desired that. We really just started walking down different paths. Resisting the temptation to drink, I prioritize my healing. This left me with a problem; I would have to either learn how to podcast alone or find guests. Initially, I attempted solitude, but it proved unsuccessful. My hats off to those who can. I started searching out to find guests and found veteran musicians and other podcasters. I truly feel like I found an entire community of support. I discovered like-minded individuals who shared my passion for podcasting. Discussing my journey and healing with them was important.

Let's assess successes and areas requiring attention. By showing families how PTSD changes you, this book aims to provide perspective. Trust and anger were still my biggest problems. My temper flares in Walmart when someone stops abruptly in the aisle. There was a shift in my attitude and desire to heal. I was unaware of some things. The fundamental question is, how do I reach my destination? What does it mean to heal? I did not like the method the VA used; it was not the right path. The issue was I did not understand the method. Just so everyone knows, the problem isn't the method the VA uses; it's the way it's delivered. Not knowing the questions prevented me from starting the process. This brings me to Season 2 of my podcast or my therapy, however you want to look at it. This was therapy, not just a podcast. I felt with a podcast you cared how many views you had; Did not matter to me if it was 1 or 10,000. I just knew it was helping me, and I wanted to keep doing it.

Chapter 13: The Unspoken Dialogue: Confronting the Inner Battle

To help you understand why I call this chapter the conversation that is ignored. The term elephant in the room signifies a problem avoided in conversation. I was aware of its presence. Season 2 of the podcast was about bringing on more guests. I came across a podcast called Contagion Effect Podcast. They reached out to me and had me on the show. The nerves hit me as a first-time show guest. The camera shows a different perspective. I was not the best guest; my answers were short, and I had a lot of defense mechanisms up and armed. This resulted in the guests I needed for my show. The first one being Scotty Hasting. His presence as a guest was remarkable, and his story left a deep impact. I will not share it here, because it's not my story to tell. This led me to another problem I discovered and wished to aid with. These musicians were depending on interviews and connections to get gigs. It's their only means of earning a living. Despite the challenge of gaining online visibility, it didn't concern me. I felt a desire to help fix this problem and built a radio station for veteran musicians. Gun Room Radio, the radio station, connected me with even more remarkable people. The family of Operation Encore filled a void in my life, giving me purpose once more. As season 2 continued, I met several guests and was enjoying my journey as a podcaster. The next part of the podcasting that changed my life was when I had Rick Yee on my show. I had learned about his program called The Warrior's Way Mindset. He later reached out to me and invited me to join his program. Attending one session, I finally felt at home.

I knew it was the perfect program for me. They would show me things here. I could not figure out what it was because I was it. The one thing I avoided was discussing myself all this time. I joined the army as one version of Donald Dunn; over the years, I became a different version, learning about who we were and our defense mechanisms. The problem was I didn't know the inner me. When we got to that point of the therapy, it was hard. Knowing thyself was the hardest part of the class. It exposes the truth of your identity, and not all of it is attractive. I held much resentment towards that person and his deeds. I had not truly forgiven myself and did not want to deal with it. That is why the meds helped. It kept that person locked up inside, but the problem was you cannot flourish like that. Knowing and accepting my past, I had to move forward. That started by forgiving myself. It allowed me to focus on changing the future and fixing the things that contributed to disliking that person. The first for me was my anger. Resentment consumed me, directed at others and myself. The day I confronted and embraced my actions was truly great. Each session I took part in improved my well-being. It is difficult, but it is worth the work you put in. Therapy's success hinges on your readiness to put in the work. This occurs at varying times for individuals. It is not one size fits all. The other issue is how it's delivered. Deliver information so the other person can receive it. Without that, everything will be for nothing. Align the two for life transformation. Podcasting brought this to my life. It is truly impressive to find individuals like Rick Yee. I wouldn't be here today without it. I owe that to podcasting.

With going through that program, I could focus more deeply on myself. That led me to apologizing to my son for how I treated him. It allowed me to write the first version of this book for just my kids and my wife, giving them the explanation they were deserving of. It led to the radio station growing and reaching thousands of people. While surrounded by veterans, I acquired the skill to fix things. Since then, I have gotten my temper more under control. I am not saying that it's fixed; this will always be a process. I am currently medicated. I still have issues with my memory, and it's gotten worse since then. Over time, the podcast has grown into a full-fledged start of a nonprofit.

I have started what is called Heroes Voice Media Foundation. The goal is to help veterans and dependents of veterans use media to tell their stories and find help they may or may not know they are searching for. Podcasting was for me; however, we offer podcasting, music, and writing with our programs. Hopefully, there are individuals with a story similar to mine among the thousands of people we are reaching. The radio station is up to 3 stations and having DJs with several people connecting with new connections through it. We have had artists invited to Zack Brown's camp, Southern Ground. We have great partnerships with amazing organizations. Prioritizing help for many individuals. It has helped me in many indescribable ways.

Learning to fix and remove negativity in life promotes daily growth. People look at healing as a disease. I want to share my healing and happiness with you. Although some days are good, there are still days when I struggle with anxiety. I still have days where I hear that inner self telling me I am a failure. Occasionally have dreams about the events that happened to me. Unsure of a permanent solution to remove it. These are aspects of the new me, just who I am. I've learned to accept and control these things, living as normally as possible. Areas needing improvement involve difficulty collaborating with others. I feel uncomfortable and don't like crowds. The job I have requires us to wear a respirator. When talking, place your face close to the person you're speaking with. This is a problem for me. I don't like people right next to me. I like my distance from other people.

This has been a struggle for me. I still struggle with communicating with non-military individuals. Occasionally, I am not very Human Resources friendly. Even now, I won't drive over dead animals or road garbage. Seeing these objects on the road still reminds me of IEDs. Sympathy is still difficult for me. This includes me as well. It's challenging, and it affects others as well. It would be false to say I'm great and healed. I've learned to accept and think more clearly, still a work in progress.

Chapter 14: The Power of Voice: Rebuilding Identity After Service

As I mentioned in the last chapter, I have built a nonprofit. I am proud of this and hope it helps others as it has helped me. Concluding this book, I want to expand on some points.

Heroes Voice Media Foundation helps keep veterans talking. I know how veterans isolate themselves and how hard it is to get them to talk. I don't think podcasting is direct therapy; however, I believe that once you talk about things that are bothering you, it's important to keep that conversation going. I have options for support, including a podcast group and understanding friends I can call. Podcasting is very competitive and very easy to quit. Once that happens, the conversation ends. We help promote them and encourage them to keep going, giving them some quick wins and talking to them to show them they have a person who will listen. We created the radio station for a different reason. Even though music is very therapeutic, it is also a very brutal industry. To sustain themselves, artists must be on a stage to earn money. We created the radio station to help them make these connections. Last, we created our author program to help veterans get their story out. Engaging in writing, which is a lonely job, frequently results in isolation. The one difference is that authors have gotten to where they feel they need to tell their story. Our role is to aid in their worldwide dissemination.

While constantly belittling myself, leaving the military stripped me of any meaningful identity. The reality of it happening was post-military. I feel passionately that our time serving this country, for the good and the bad, is a huge part of our identity. As veterans, we can no longer rely on historians to tell our story; we need to do it. These programs, whether through podcasting, songwriting, or authorship, offer perspectives on how the Middle East experienced. You are getting a piece of the identity of that veteran.

During this part of my life, building my identity was happening. I had to forgive my old self and embrace the new me. The things in earlier chapters are unchangeable, as they are my history. Those things don't define me. I, like everyone else, have experienced hardships. I remember having a guest on my show who was part of the British army. During the conversation, he mentioned something at the end of his current show. This show was a mental health-themed show, because of the number of soldiers killing themselves. This hit me like a ton of bricks. I never thought suicide would affect veterans from other nations. From my perspective, this has always been a concern for American veterans. This is a human problem. Things you read in this book are nothing different from any other person. Occupation doesn't determine who can have PTSD. Triggers and responses are the only variables.

Seeing current events in our country will clarify this understanding. Trauma doesn't resolve like a common cold. Dedicate effort and observe these things. It will always remain within you. While writing this book, I have much progress ahead. I'm working on fixing these issues. I have forgiven myself for the things that I have done. Through the book, my family gains an understanding of my experiences and motivations. I am not writing this book to get forgiveness or sympathy. I write to convey the experience of individuals with PTSD, including their families. Everything I've done shaped who I am now. I can finally accept myself when I look in the mirror.

I have spoken with several other veterans who are fighting their own demons and have podcasted. Veterans that continue to do it have told me it helps. The power of giving back is also therapy. The hope that most veterans podcasting have is to tell their story, hoping it reaches just one person and helps improve their life. This does not mean if you do this, you're healed. No shortcuts. Work is required. Next chapter will cover the work and my accomplishments.

All the programs I use have to be used when you are ready. I started podcasting with the thought I was ready to help others. Another part of me grew tired of my current existence. After telling the Turbine 33 story, I felt prepared to seek help and navigate my life's struggles. I opted for the lengthier path. Most of us aren't. I believe the nonprofit benefits me more than I contribute. It's selfish of me to prioritize getting through this and rebuilding my life. As there is no magic formula or cute saying, I cannot assist you in descending these steps. It starts by deciding you are worth fighting for and want to live. I made that decision during the first season of our podcast. Steps silenced the voice inside, deeming me worthless. As I did these things, I took one step forward, then another. Steps get easier. I won't quit until I regain my life. If you establish your foundation, you will have a solid ground. Heroes Voice Media Foundation may not be your answer, but it's one example of hundreds of choices that you can use to help you walk down those steps. That just was my path.

Chapter 15: The Conversation Ignored: Unveiling the Struggle Within

If you're reading this book, I'm going to assume that either you are living with someone you think has PTSD, or you have PTSD yourself. I'm no doctor, nor am I offering any kind of medical advice. Being a veteran, I made an early career choice, thinking I could bear that burden for my family. I didn't want my family to witness evil beyond the monster under your bed. I refrained from discussing overseas experiences, unaware of the many deployments and stories that would follow. Would talking about it have caused a divorce because my wife couldn't carry that burden? Could my wife and I have been closer under different circumstances? I'm unsure, and I believe this is a question individuals must answer. I chose, now I live and deal with the consequences. I'm writing this book hoping it might help someone recognize these types of situations and understand what's happening. It doesn't mean that knowing someone has PTSD instantly fixes it, but it means understanding that the situation isn't your fault, and the behaviors are not because of you. This insight can be helpful for both you and the person battling these demons. Perhaps if my wife had told me I needed help sooner, I wouldn't have made some choices I did. But was I ready to listen? I don't know, and it likely would have led to a fight had it happened.

The individual experiencing this fights an invisible war. They don't understand it, nor do they know the rules. Clear rules governed combat; unlike dealing with depression. I never thought I would become that guy. Reflecting, I notice how I shifted from military companions to intentionally avoiding family. I'm sure my wife noticed these changes. Mental health never crossed our minds. I was unaware of PTSD symptoms until I received help. The day I sat down and read about it, I showed it to my wife and asked who it sounded like. She read it and said it sounded like me. Realizing something was wrong, I felt the need to change, yet I was unaware of the extent of what it would entail or fully understand the internal turmoil I was experiencing.

Knowing your past is essential to understanding your present self. It won't be everything you want to hear, but it will help you move forward if you keep your ears open and listen to what you're telling yourself. Initially, it's hard to tell what's going on, at least for myself. Inexperienced with medication, and disliking drugs, things improved, but I lacked guidance on coping. I took my meds, and the anxiety went down. While my wife saw improvements, I merely paused the war in my head. The war persisted despite the paused fight. Medication helps stabilize, but without a skilled psychologist and therapist, guidance is unclear.

I used that time to reconcile with my family, avoiding discussions about the past. Joking about meds and being nuts made me feel good. Despite my efforts, I could not repair the growing distance between my wife and me, and not all of it was solely my responsibility, although I probably played a part.

My wife has always been shy and close to me. As I drifted apart, she had to become more independent, taking care of our kids and herself. I'm not proud of that, but not everything you hear about yourself will be pleasant. That contributed significantly to our divide. I won't go into details about other aspects, as that's her story to tell, not mine. It's important to understand that just because you have PTSD, it doesn't mean the resulting problems are entirely your fault. Please consider yourself and the bigger picture, something I hesitated to do, and others may feel the same.

Being able to differentiate when to be compassionate and when to push someone forward is key in supporting them. My wife had no issue with this, particularly the latter. Not providing both can lead to falling into a victim's role. When I started learning about PTSD, I felt like everything afterward was because of it. This mindset will not help you move forward; it's a spot you don't want to stay in for long. I learned you start not taking responsibility for anything you say or do. Admitting and facing what you have done is an important part of healing. Until you can forgive yourself, you won't start liking or loving yourself, and if you can't, how can you expect others to?

Discussing the inner thoughts is vital. We often refer to battling inner demons for a reason. I could hear myself berating my worth, leading to thoughts of how life would be better if I were dead. Feeling like everything was against me, my confidence plummeted to barely functioning. This internal war is invisible to others, who may see only anger or withdrawn behavior, not the battle raging within. Therefore, you can't fight this alone and why isolation is a common response. These demons want you isolated; they know victory comes through teamwork. When I reached out for help, I had already isolated myself in a semi-truck, feeling anxious about going back home because these demons made me believe I wasn't wanted there. Little Anne, my dog, was the only comfort that understood and did not judge. Those moments of connection felt good, emphasizing the struggle against an unseen enemy.

Reaching rock bottom but still alive, deciding to seek help was the first correct decision I had made since leaving the army. At that juncture, the ultimate choice emerges: to live or to die. Subconsciously, I wanted to live, but the demons convinced me otherwise, to the point of planning my demise, finding solace only in thoughts of death. Explaining this to someone who hasn't shared your pain or can relate to your experiences is challenging. After enough judgment, you stop talking. Soldiers have even told me about being judged for using an accessible parking spot without a visible injury, revealing how society has constructed a perception of what disability should appear as. Everything I've described can disable, and it doesn't take much to validate the voices that undermine you. Someone's judgment can provoke actions.

Seeking help marked the beginning of a journey to a better life. The path involves acknowledging your worth and deciding to live, a decision I made during the first season of our podcast. As I take each step forward, the journey gradually becomes easier, and I persistently remind myself that I won't give up until I reclaim my life. Heroes Voice Media Foundation may not be the answer for everyone, but it's one of many options that can help guide you through your journey. It just was my path.

Chapter 16: The Journey Through Shadows: Toward Light and Understanding

Starting as a brief documentation of my experiences for my family, this book has developed into something much larger. A lingering question in my journey was whether I should have discussed with my wife the things that were happening, especially the depression I was feeling. Perhaps, had I shared more, this book could have been shorter. At this point in my life, I realize I was not alone in withholding these stories. There are others out there experiencing similar challenges with no one around them understanding what's happening.

Readers should take away insights into improving awareness and educating others. If you recall, I was once the guy who loved making everyone laugh. Throughout the 29 years covered in this book, both my wife and I have changed. It's uncertain if she noticed my mood shifts and the gradual changes in my behavior. The changes did not occur suddenly.

Another significant change was my desire to always be around my family. Having been with my wife since junior high and experiencing the joy of becoming a parent, I valued my family deeply. Despite the passing years, I've continued to feel uneasy around them. I can't fully explain it, but it's very real. On the surface, this discomfort seems nonsensical, but it becomes clearer when you consider the cumulative effects of repeated deployments.

My cognitive abilities have also changed. I used to excel in math and enjoyed poker because of my knack for calculating odds. Over time, however, my ability to perform mental math has diminished, and my memory has significantly suffered. I struggle to recall what my children looked like as youngsters, which leads me to question my adequacy as a father. It's unclear whether these issues stem from medication, a Traumatic Brain Injury (TBI), or both, but the frustration is palpable when searching for words that escape me. This affects my work, and my wife has noticed my failing memory, perhaps thinking it was intentional. Unless they take trauma from deployments into consideration, people often disregard these cognitive changes as the effects of aging or stress.

My drinking habits changed subtly over the years. I shifted from beer to mostly liquor, with the amount and frequency of my drinking increasing. While I wasn't drinking to get drunk, it helped take the edge off and aided my sleep. The worst times were quiet nights when the demons in my head screamed. Even though I didn't drink on the road, sleeplessness was a common occurrence.

Sleep disturbances are perhaps the clearest indicator that something is amiss. My wife definitely noticed problems related to my experiences overseas, moving out of our bed because of my physical reactions during sleep and my night-time vocalizations. Despite her inquiries, I insisted nothing was wrong, believing I was making the right choice for myself by not discussing it. However, communication is crucial, and I now realize the importance of not letting things build up internally. Being in a supportive environment where I can share and combat these internal struggles has played a significant role in my recovery.

Recognizing someone's transformation and loving them in their current state is equally important as loving their past self. Rewiring the brain from its conditioned responses takes time and understanding. Throughout this journey, I've come to understand the significance of being present and cherishing each moment, as life's beauty frequently exists in these fleeting instances.

About the Author

I served 20 Years in the military. 68 Months spent in Iraq and Afghanistan and Bosnia.

My main focus is on our Non Profit helping veterans use Media as therapy.

Read more at https://www.wordsfromwarriors.org.

www.ingramcontent.com/pod-product-compliance
Lightning Source LLC
Chambersburg PA
CBHW060447160726
47992CB00003B/1117